Writing with the bold urgency of a prophet and the tender heart of a pastor, Marlena offers her readers an evocative image: You and I are called to become little boats bearing the compassionate presence of Christ into the uncharted waters of our bruised and broken world. To help us respond faithfully to this calling, she offers us navigational instructions that are accessible, practical, and helpful for our voyage. Reading her words with my South African eyes, I valued her constant emphasis on our Christ following being related to personal engagement with those who suffer around us. The generous glimpses Marlena shares of her own voyaging experiences give her written words the ring of deep authenticity and genuineness.

TREVOR HUDSON, pastor in the Methodist Church of Southern Africa and author of *Seeking God: Finding Another Kind of Life with St. Ignatius and Dallas Willard*

Take your time reading *Bearing God* because author Marlena Graves invites us into the slow, ongoing work of soul formation. Graves reminds us that it is not enough to know or believe but that in a noisy world our actions speak loudly about the God whose image we bear.

KATHY KHANG, writer, speaker, and yoga teacher

What a captivating reflection by acclaimed theologian Marlena Graves, who asks what it would mean to be the little boat humbly carrying a restful Jesus across the raging storms of our lives in service to others. Could you fill that role? Could I? Her enchanting musings serve as an enthralling guide to exploring such a remarkable question. Brief and brilliant, *Bearing God* is a totally lovely manual for the thoughtful and brave.

PATRICIA RAYBON, Christy Award–winni
Mysteries and *I Told the Mountain to Move: L*

Living a
Christ-Formed Life
in Uncharted Waters

Bearing
God

MARLENA
GRAVES

A NavPress resource published in alliance
with Tyndale House Publishers

NavPress is the publishing ministry of The Navigators, an international Christian organization and leader in personal spiritual development. NavPress is committed to helping people grow spiritually and enjoy lives of meaning and hope through personal and group resources that are biblically rooted, culturally relevant, and highly practical.

For more information, visit NavPress.com.

Bearing God: Living a Christ-Formed Life in Uncharted Waters

Copyright © 2023 by Marlena Graves. All rights reserved.

A NavPress resource published in alliance with Tyndale House Publishers

NavPress and the NavPress logo are registered trademarks of NavPress, The Navigators, Colorado Springs, CO. *Tyndale* is a registered trademark of Tyndale House Ministries. Absence of ® in connection with marks of NavPress or other parties does not indicate an absence of registration of those marks.

The Team:
David Zimmerman, Publisher; Caitlyn Carlson, Acquisitions Editor; Deborah Sáenz Gonzalez, Developmental Editor; Elizabeth Schroll, Copy Editor; Olivia Eldredge, Operations Manager; Julie Chen, Designer; Sarah K. Johnson, Proofreading Coordinator

Cover images are the property of their respective copyright holders from Adobe Stock, and all rights are reserved. Storm on the sea oil painting © vladnikon; canoe paddles © MarekPhotoDesign.com; wooden boat © kontur-vid; canvas texture © Mehmet Gokhan Bayhan; oars © Javvani.

Author photo by Courtney Ranes Photography, copyright © 2022. All rights reserved.

Author is represented by The Christopher Ferebee Agency, www.christopherferebee.com

All Scripture quotations, unless otherwise indicated, are taken from the Holy Bible, *New International Version,*® *NIV.*® Copyright © 1973, 1978, 1984, 2011 by Biblica, Inc.® Used by permission. All rights reserved worldwide. Scripture quotations marked KJV are taken from the *Holy Bible*, King James Version.

Some of the anecdotal illustrations in this book are true to life and are included with the permission of the persons involved. All other illustrations are composites of real situations, and any resemblance to people living or dead is purely coincidental.

For information about special discounts for bulk purchases, please contact Tyndale House Publishers at csresponse@tyndale.com, or call 1-855-277-9400.

ISBN 978-1-64158-623-8

Printed in the United States of America

29	28	27	26	25	24	23
7	6	5	4	3	2	1

For Mami, Myrna Proper (Deida Ramos-Negron)

May 3, 1946–June 27, 2021

You are the love of my life. And you loved us well, as best as you could. Thank you. We all miss you more than words can reveal. We are who we are because of you and dad and the great cloud of witnesses. I hope this makes you proud while in paradise with God.

Contents

JOURNEY WITH JESUS INTO UNCHARTED WATERS

A ship in harbor is safe, but that is not what ships are built for.

JOHN A. SHEDD

MY MOTHER IS DEAD. I sit all alone in the pew of the sun-lit, pristine white sanctuary of Saint John XXIII during a Saturday evening mass in July. The décor is minimalist, and the otherworldly brightness of the sanctuary as the sun streams in through the windows makes me think about the description of Jesus' clothing during the Transfiguration: "His clothes became as white as the light" (Matthew 17:2). No one here knows who I am. No one knows I have spent close to ten months on rotation with my three siblings nursing Mami before and during hospice care. It's as if we were all suspended in time during Mami's final days. Time slowed to molasses, allowing us to enjoy our last moments with her while trying to figure out how to help our father cope.

After every treatment, the poison from radiation and chemotherapy sent her into the ER. So she chose to stop it so she could die in our presence. Had she continued the treatment and remained in the hospital, COVID-19 restrictions would have allowed just my dad and sister to visit her. No one else. She wanted to see her children, husband, and grandchildren in her last days. I remember the doctor saying that she had never seen a family care so well for one of her patients and for each other. I was shocked by her words, because—after all—what else would a family do? My attention returns to the service. No one has any idea what I've just gone through. And thus, nobody has the opportunity to care, to shoulder my sadnesses. But I am here to be close to Mami—to my childhood.

Blinking in the sunlight streaming through the windows and onto my face, I sit, tired and weary from what the world has laid on me. Thoughts swirl around in my head like thousands of falling leaves being tossed around and around, to and fro, this way and that, playing in a forest unsettled by autumn wind gusts. As I am playing catch-them-if-you-can with my thoughts, my reverie is interrupted again as the congregation stands in unison to listen to the priest read the Gospel lesson. Today's passage is from the book of Mark, chapter 4, where Jesus is asleep in the boat as it is tossed about by the storm's furies.

Reflections on Jesus' first nature miracle often focus on

Jesus' ability to calm the storm despite the disciples' lack of faith. This miracle demonstrates Jesus' divinity; even the foul weather and menacing waves obey him. It also reminds us of our humanity. Just as we are prone to do, the disciples fail to realize that wherever they are with Jesus, they are truly safe. There is no need to fear. I once heard Dallas Willard say, "The Kingdom of God is the safest place on earth." This begs the question *Then whom or what shall we fear?*

As I sat erect, concentrating on the passage as Father Herb read from Mark 4, I immediately found myself immersed in the story. But this time I was not one of the terrified disciples lacking faith, wondering if I was going to drown and miffed at Jesus for remaining asleep and undisturbed by the perilous storm—oblivious of our impending doom. Neither was I Jesus, exhausted down to the marrow of my bones, so tired from ministry that I peacefully slept through danger—even though I was terrifically exhausted. Nor was I the wind or the waves.

No, during this reading, in what was one of the biggest surprises of my life, God impressed upon me that I was the little fishing boat carrying Jesus in the storm. A tiny vessel in an uproarious storm on the great Sea of Galilee! Call me the *Santa Marlena*. Up and down I went as waves crashed into me. I rolled to one side, then to another. The disciples furiously scrambled to keep me from capsizing. All the while Jesus was sleeping like a baby, without a care in the world. I had certainly never imagined myself being the Jesus boat. As I sat in shock, it occurred to me that, like Jesus' mother,

Mary, and like a fishing boat in which Jesus curls up to sleep, I, too, am a God bearer. As I set out to sea, or make my way back into port, I carry Jesus. Indeed, we are all Marys, or in this case, all little vessels carrying Jesus as we journey throughout our lives. That is, of course, unless we send him overboard, ejecting him from his resting place.

That evening, I savored the thoughts of being the little boat and kept them close to my heart. Later in the night during my evening prayers, and in the context of my epiphany, some of the implications of being the boat began dawning on me. First and foremost was the reality that as a Jesus boat, I would have to traverse stormy seas. It seems obvious given the passage in Mark 4, but I had not extended my imagination beyond bearing Christ until then. And so, after the thought occurred to me, I spoke up: *I am tired and weary. If I am the boat, keep me docked close to shore.* I continued, *Let me rest. No more sea voyages for me for a while. No more hard assignments, please.* Perhaps my words were motivated by a different exhaustion than Jesus'. His exhaustion from ministry allowed him to sleep peacefully through the storm. My exhaustion resulted from being tossed, bruised, and battered by the vicissitudes of life as I sought to journey with Jesus. Well, maybe our exhaustion wasn't so different after all. What I really wanted was to bear God for a spell while tethered to the shore in a safe harbor as the waves gently lapped the shore. Maybe change careers and become a tugboat or a ferry that takes passengers back and forth across the bay. I wanted God to call a time-out for me from storms so I could

It occurred to me that,
like Jesus' mother, Mary,
and like a fishing boat in which
Jesus curls up to sleep, I, too,
am a God bearer.

avoid hurricanes and squalls. Semiretirement from difficulties. After all, I have faithfully put my time in.

Of course, God promptly responded to me during our evening conversation. It was basically *No can do.* He told me that boats are not made to remain tethered to the shore but to go out to sea. I understood that "going out to sea" meant embracing God's will for my life instead of refusing it. He kindly reminded me that I am not the captain of the ship, nor the captain of my soul. God is the captain of the ship and my soul, despite what William Ernest Henley's poem "Invictus" might have me believe: "I thank whatever gods may be / For my unconquerable soul. . . . I am the master of my fate, / I am the captain of my soul."[1] However, God, as captain, has always been one to take input from lowly me and others—contrary to what some theologians might have us believe. God takes our desires into consideration, so I felt the freedom to let him know my opinion. Did not Abraham negotiate with God about Sodom and Gomorrah? Then I, too, could enter negotiations.

A month or so later, while the idea of me being the little fishing boat carrying a resting Jesus in me marinated within my soul, I stumbled upon John A. Shedd's coincidentally similar observation about a ship's purpose: "A ship in harbor is safe, but that is not what ships are built for." *Okay, Lord. I get the message loud and clear.* How very like God to underscore the point—just in case I didn't get it the first time around.

LED BY LOVE OF GOD AND NEIGHBOR

*Holiness consists simply in doing God's will
and being just what God wants us to be.*

SAINT THÉRÈSE OF LISIEUX

IF I AM SAILING OUT TO SEA bearing Christ in me, what do I need to know? Besides needing to recognize the fact that there will be many a fierce and sudden storm, I need navigation instructions. To know God's will. *Just where are you taking me, Jesus?*

At its most basic (and yet perhaps most difficult) level, God's will for us is that we love God with everything we are and love our neighbors as ourselves. That's Sunday School Answer 101. But it's one thing to give the correct answer and another thing to do it. Following through on loving God and our neighbors isn't so easy. How, in fact, do we love God? We can only learn to love God when we behold God and allow ourselves to be beheld by God. And when we are held and beheld by God and we behold him, we come to delight in and enjoy God while being transformed into his likeness. We become deliriously happy in one another, deeply in love and in joy with one another. Perhaps we serenade God with The Flamingos' classic hit "I Only Have Eyes for You."[1] We tell him we have no other gods before him and mean it. All else falls away from view and priority when we are held and beheld. We are in the utmost reality and see with clarity.

God never takes his eyes off us. Never. We are the apple of his eye. His joy is to be in our presence. And we are transformed in his. That is why Dallas Willard could say that the Kingdom of God is the safest place on earth. God does no evil, only good. Neither is God the author of evil in our lives or elsewhere on the earth or in the universe.

What keeps us enamored with Christ, our eyes glued to him? We simply do it, with his help. Enamored with Christ is exactly what we must be. And our being follows from our doing, not our thinking. For example, my sister, Michelle, a nurse, told me about a time she was on her way home from work when she strolled by a couple of pulmonologists (lung doctors) she knew as she left the hospital and made her way to her car in the parking lot. They were standing outside smoking. She could not stop cackling because of the irony of what she observed. These doctors "know" all there is to know about lung disease and the deleterious effects of smoking, but knowing doesn't necessitate acting accordingly. This is an example of how our being doesn't always follow from our thinking; rather, our being follows from our doing.

We can only learn to love God when we behold God and allow ourselves to be beheld by God.

We can know that we should trust Jesus, but that is different than actively putting our trust in Jesus. Having a rational understanding of something has little effect unless our knowledge results in doing. So, for me, and historically for the church throughout the ages, trusting God means meditating on his Word and being in community with other believers who are also striving to trust God through their being and doing. It is also being still and knowing that God is God (Psalm 46:10). I do that by being out in nature, not overscheduling myself, serving the poor and the marginalized, giving what I have to those who need it, concretely loving my family and those close to me, and fasting from social media. As I do that, I begin to know what it means to live.

No matter how much time I spend thinking about going out to sea, or doing God's will, it is not the same as *actually* going out to sea. There is a world of difference between my imagination concerning God's will and the reality of doing God's will. The main difference is embodiment. Actually putting one foot right in front of the other. Not merely having good intentions. So I have to set my sights on Christ that I might do, know, and be—that I might head to his destination for this journey. To be clear: Our knowing comes from our doing, and then our being follows. Setting our eyes on Christ enables us to filter our thoughts, actions, and dispositions through his eyes and heart. We do (doing), and then we are enlightened (knowing), and then we are transformed (being).

As we progressively become more like Christ, we see more clearly and treat others more rightly—the way Jesus sees and treats them. Our posture toward and treatment of others, especially those closest to us, those with whom we live and work and play, is a good indicator of the level of our transformation, of our doing God's will. It's often easier to treat people with whom we have little interaction well than those with whom we regularly interact. There isn't much of a chance for those we rarely encounter to get on our nerves or push our buttons. The real test of our love and transformation is how we treat those closest to us when there is no chance to put on a pious show for others. Kinship with others flows out of our relationship with God. We realize that we are our brothers' and sisters' keepers—and the earth's. That is God's plan. Anything else is *Invictus-ing*—a deviation from God's will, a running off course, and an entanglement with death (Psalm 18:4). No *Invictus-ing* for us, lest we leave destruction in our wake and run aground.

It is so simple. But not. For some reason, the simplest things, the basics in life—eating well, exercising regularly, getting plenty of sleep, and not overscheduling ourselves—can be difficult. We are comfortable with ill health and dysfunction because health requires exertion, sacrifice, and changing our habits. Similarly, loving God with all we are and loving our neighbors as ourselves, which make for wholeness (Hebrew *shalom*), can be difficult to learn. At least at first. At least without the help of the Holy Spirit and wise friends. Or within a toxic church culture.

When we set out to sea, there will be many uncertainties, but thankfully, we have our navigation instructions to help lead the way. How do we know if we are headed in the right direction? If we truly love God, and if Jesus is indeed within us, then as my husband, Shawn, says, "We should be bothered if our neighbors are not flourishing."

Some of us are not bothered by our neighbors' lack of flourishing. Thus, it follows that we are lying or engaged in self-deception when we maintain that we love God. We know that we do not love God when we do not love our neighbors (1 John 4:20). It is not enough to love our neighbors in our imaginations. If asked, would our neighbors testify to us loving and caring for them, or would they testify to our lack of love and concern for them? Or would they do us a favor and use their right to remain silent—with the silence speaking volumes about our failure to love them?

Not long ago, I was teaching an undergraduate class, and the day's topic was abortion. That day, I was explaining the lay of the land, talking about the number of abortion clinics and the meaning of the word *viability*. I also highlighted the cost of raising a child to age eighteen in different parts of the US. Most of my students were freshmen and sophomores, though I had a few juniors and seniors sprinkled in.

Throughout the semester, I'd repeatedly reminded my students that people have reasons for holding their views and that although we might not agree with a person's views, we should listen to them and seek to understand where they're coming from. Thankfully, students abided by these classroom norms. Many testified to feeling safe enough to express their opinions in my class even if others disagreed with them because the disagreement was respectful. What I found profoundly interesting each time I did the unit on abortion is that students across the value spectrum considered the fetus a baby. A child. They did not argue about the humanity of the baby, though they disagreed on when life begins. I encouraged students to listen to those whose views on abortion fell in a different place on the spectrum than their own, because those students had well-thought-out reasons for their beliefs. What we should not do was demonize one another.

As students registered their opinions on the abortion debate, one student spoke up. "I had an abortion," she said. "There's no way I could have continued going to college if I'd had a baby. My boyfriend and I can't afford to raise a child." The class grew silent; some students stared down at their desks, and others stared off into space. Some fiddled with their cell phones. Others turned around to look at the student as she spoke. She continued. "My parents tried to talk me out of it." And then she laid it all out. "I asked if they were going to babysit the baby while I was at school and work. If they were going to purchase clothing and formula and help with whatever bills insurance did not cover. If they were going to help put money away for the baby's college tuition and help with miscellaneous expenses. I also wanted to know if they would vote for laws that give mothers and children a stronger safety net *after the child is born* instead of just being pro-birth."

Then—having established almost a semester's worth of credibility and trust with the class—I asked, "Do you mind telling us what they said? Of course, you don't have to answer this question if it makes you uncomfortable." Students could always opt out of answering questions in my class. I have had students elect not to answer specific questions or participate in certain discussions before. What transpired seemed like an eternal pause. I waited with bated breath. Counted to ten. I had no idea what to expect. Then she said, "They did not say much except that they could not commit to all those things. Obviously, it was too much. So I had the abortion. Like I said, my boyfriend and I can't afford a baby right now." And then she added, "Pro-birth people talk a good game, but they don't want to support mothers and children once the babies are born." I was stunned. All I could do is offer my deepest thanks to her for so bravely entrusting us with such intimate details.

Really, I could not argue with her. She was 100 percent right. We Christians in the US would have to vote differently to care for mothers, children, and families for our pro-life stance to be credible. Hold our representatives' feet to the fire. Hold the fathers' feet to the fire. Childcare and medical care are expensive. Housing is expensive. Diapers and formula are expensive. Folks need more of a safety net— truly pro-life policies—in place. Not only would we have to pay more taxes to be concretely pro-life, but most of us would also have to simplify our lifestyles and pay more out-of-pocket expenses to support mothers and children. Being truly pro-life may mean taking in a mother and baby to help them get on their feet. Or perhaps creating a special fund in our churches to support them.

Love is action oriented; it is not merely running our mouths. And we are good at running our mouths. If we continue to live as we are—just talk, talk, talk, talk, talk and do lots of Bible study and memorization without application—we will become *those* people, the type James speaks so strongly about in his epistle: "Suppose a brother or a sister is without clothes and daily food. If one of you says to them, 'Go in peace; keep warm and well fed,' but does nothing about their physical needs, what good is it? In the same way, faith by itself, if it is not accompanied by action, is dead" (James 2:15-17). Christian activist and journalist Dorothy Day nailed it when she put it this way: "I have long since come to believe that people never mean half of what they say, and that it is best to disregard their talk and judge only their actions."[2] That's what my student was doing—judging by her parents' action (or rather, inaction). She felt that having an abortion was the only option, the only way to take responsibility for her own behavior. She did not want to raise a child in poverty. What would we say if my student put the question to us? Do *our* actions vindicate our words?

Loving God and loving neighbors—God's will for us—often requires inconvenient sacrifices. And, not surprisingly, it is the mundane inconveniences that we most often wish to avoid. To flee. After all, they are not dramatic. Exciting. Sensational. Sacrifice often means that we are not the center of attention or consideration; other people are. It is in the daily inconveniences, the daily difficulties, the interruptions that C. S. Lewis rightly called our "life,"[3] where the chance to show love to our neighbors occurs. Jesus, the Lord of all that is unimaginably glorious, is also the master of loving people in the mundane.

Of course, there *could* be great heroics involved in loving our neighbors, like the way a soldier saves a friend (or perhaps an enemy) or the way a parent gives their life for a child. It could be displaying heroic love for God while standing on a beach as one of the twenty-one martyrs, mostly poor migrants, whose blood stained the blue Mediterranean Sea red after an extremist group murdered them for refusing to denounce Christ.[4] (May their memory be eternal, as the Eastern Orthodox say.)

Plenty of us Christians imagine ourselves being willing to die for Christ in a blaze of glory, but few of us are willing to live for him. Beware of those who preach that Christianity is primarily "doing great and mighty things for God"—exhibiting public heroics, like growing a church by the thousands . . . only for thousands to be disillusioned and fall away when we tumble down, down, down because we are putting on a show. Yes, let us also be careful of doing "mighty things" for God when God merely asks us to do little things with great love, as Mother Teresa pointed out.[5] *Consistently loving in the little things is the great thing.* The mighty thing. Unimaginably glorious. We can only ever hope to be faithful in much when we are faithful in little (Luke 16:10). How do you think Jesus could torturously eke out "Father, forgive them; for they know not what they do" while fading toward death on the cross (Luke 23:34, KJV)? It may be that it's only because he had practiced forgiving his enemies on a regular basis throughout his lifetime *before* he was crucified. He wasn't going to do in crucifixion what he didn't do in life.

Being good at being great can be tragic if it comes at the cost of everything and everyone around us. Unfortunately, much of the time we do not realize this cost until damage has been done. And some of that damage is irreparable. Is that God's will—to achieve while doing damage to others, ourselves, or the earth? Nah. It's hard to follow Jesus when we have too much stuff and when we have stuffed too many activities into our lives because we are shackled to the American markers of success, status, and comfort.

Achievement must be reined in. Relationships must be reined in. Everything should be within bounds. Maybe Ecclesiastes was born of a midlife crisis. Having experienced much, maybe the philosopher had his own version, an ancient yet evergreen version, of John Cougar Mellencamp's "Oh yeah, life goes on, long after the thrill of livin' is gone."[6] No wonder he declared, "Remember your Creator in the days of your youth, before the days of trouble come and the years approach when you will say, 'I find no pleasure in them.' . . . 'Meaningless! Meaningless!' says the Teacher. 'Everything is meaningless!'" (Ecclesiastes 12:1, 8). We strive and we grasp, sometimes making ourselves and others miserable as we chase dreams of greatness only to discover that life is much more than achievement. We believe that the purpose-driven life ought to always be exciting, devoid of the mundane, and oh-so-invigorating! After all, aren't many of those on social media living it up? Compared to them, our lives may be rather boring, dastardly, and inglorious. We are tempted to reproduce others' seemingly fascinating lives. Or we despair.

We have our "Christian" versions of this. My last semester of coursework is done. So now I have a bit more time to navigate the waters of social media. What I see are commercials— Christians hawking themselves or their wares or some sort of hybrid "Christian" self-help formula, for individuals or churches, all in the name of Jesus. It's big business and big money in the Christian subculture.

Or I see so-called church leaders go to war against Christians of different persuasions because they are interested in building their little fiefdoms and want everyone else to be subject to them. Astonishing. I see no difference between the way they treat fellow Christians and the behavior of their meanest, most rabid, most foaming-at-the-mouth secular counterparts. Their posturing reveals that they are especially insecure and act out of zeal but without knowledge.

Their subcultural Christian mantra goes something like this: "Be a mean, 'manly' Christian. Say outrageous things. Tell people to buzz off. Make big pronouncements. Be an expert at everything. This is how to amass followers. Don't you know that Jesus' commandments don't apply on social media and that following them doesn't make you successful? Nice people finish last." All in the name of Jesus! For them, publicly flaying Christians they deem heretics and the pats on the back they receive from their small cadre of followers make for success. Many non-Christians behave better than they do. Theologians attribute the goodness of non-Christians to common grace. I wish such grace were more common among Christians.

All this fighting and devouring of one another is demonic. The book of James warns us, "If you harbor bitter envy and selfish ambition in your hearts, do not boast about it or deny the truth. Such 'wisdom' does not come down from heaven but is earthly, unspiritual, demonic. For where you have envy and selfish ambition, there you find disorder and every evil practice" (James 3:14-16). *Lord, have mercy!* The demonic and disorderly and all sorts of evil are manifesting in the US church through its leaders! This is neither God's will nor the way of Jesus. But it is a salient feature of American evangelical culture and in any church culture where fear, power, money, and ego are.

Flee this notion of success.

Success for God using devilish and demonic means is really the devil's success. So as we set out to sea on the journey of faith, we have to ask ourselves if we really want to do God's will—to bend to the direction of the Good Captain of our souls—or to act as if we believe the death-dealing lie that we are the captains of our souls. Do we want to do God's will always, or only when it suits us or promises commercial success or political power? We cannot go for money, fame, or power. Chasing them will corrupt us—kill us. Jesus knew

Theologians attribute the goodness of non-Christians to common grace. I wish such grace were more common among Christians.

this and resisted these temptations in the desert and over and over throughout his life (see Matthew 4 and throughout the rest of the Gospels). Money helps for sure—having a roof over our heads, electricity, food, water, clothing, and transportation—but it cannot purchase virtue, joy, happiness, or peace. Don't chase it. Of course, we need to be able to pay our bills, and if we happen to have lots of money, we will be able to give more to more of our neighbors (and keep from hoarding it for ourselves). Additionally, power can do a little, but it is still impotent to bring about the good life. And fame is fleeting and leaves many famous people lonely because they cannot always be sure whether those around them like them for who they are or for the mere bragging rights and benefits of knowing a famous person. Fame can alienate us.

If achieving worldly success costs us our health, happiness, and relationships and keeps us from loving God and our neighbors, what good is it? I write this thinking about shooting-star pastor celebrities who were going, going, and are now gone. They stepped on the backs of their people, many who cared the most about them and the mission, to reach the stars. They climbed the ladder to success on people's backs. They injured others for their selfish gain.

I think about the suicide epidemic among famous musicians.[7] Many have died at my age or just a little older. Some have been a little younger. These were people who had everything: money, power, fame, sexual freedom and allure, leisure—but none of these things were an antidote to sadness, misery, addiction, or existential angst. The pain was too much for them. They merely sought relief.

If we want to know God's will, we can know that true success is being the servant of all. Whether it results in fame or wealth or power is another thing. And if it does, we cannot revel in it or use its benefits for ourselves, lest we be destroyed. God wills for us to seek first his Kingdom and his righteousness; and then, as we participate in his divine nature, what we need for a godly life will be given to us (Matthew 6:33; 2 Peter 1:3-4).

None of us will pass life's big tests when we refuse to put in the effort in the little things (with the help of the Holy Spirit). You know who the great ones in the Kingdom are? Those who are faithful in the little. The servants of all. Those who give up their power to serve Jesus. Those we often overlook. Those who give up their power to serve the disempowered, dispossessed, and disinherited. In this way, we see that in God's Kingdom, little is much.

In a very real sense, bearing Christ entails bearing our neighbors. Saint Antony of Egypt put it this way: "We ought to love one another warmly, for he who loves his neighbour loves God, and he who loves God loves his own soul."[8] Saint Antony also stated, "From the neighbour comes life and death."[9] Our lives, the vessels in which we carry Christ and his gospel, should not be vessels of his (or anyone else's) destruction. They are to be blessings, not curses, bringing life and salvation, not death, for those who were in other vessels but have been thrown overboard.

LED BY OUR LOVES
AND JOYS

*The place God calls you to is the place where your deep gladness
and the world's deep hunger meet.*

FREDERICK BUECHNER

GOD'S WILL FOR ME AND YOU IS, of course, always connected
to the flourishing of our neighbors. That is certain. And as
we journey in our transformation into Christlikeness, we
become more and more fully human, closer to whom we are
meant to be. As Saint Irenaeus observed, "The glory of God
is a living man"—or, as others have translated it, "The glory
of God is a human being fully alive."[1]

But maybe we are wondering about direction and guidance as we go out to sea. Some of us are already loving God
and our neighbors to the best of our abilities where we are.
Like the rich young man who spoke with Jesus, we have
kept all the commandments (Matthew 19:16-20). He was

wondering what more he had to do to inherit eternal life, but we might be wondering about where we should live and whether we are to marry (and if so, whom to marry). What school should we attend, if any? Should we enter or leave ministry? Should we move back to our hometowns to take care of our parents? Should we remarry, or take the promotion, go back to school, or enter the fray? What direction shall we go as we venture out again, or maybe out for the first time? We need guidance and instruction, navigation tools.

What we need to avoid is becoming stressed out, frozen, or overwhelmed. We must not fall into despair, fearing that we will get it wrong. We can easily think that we will upset or disappoint God or our ship has already set sail and we have lost our chance to fulfill our calling (and thus are fated to a mediocre or miserable existence). God does not cruelly punish us because we make honest mistakes or don't hear him right. Jesus doesn't spend his time in our boat wagging his finger or shaking his fist at us. God is not that way. We may be waylaid for a bit, but we will never be looked down on by our Creator. Does a good and healthy parent abuse their child for not understanding instructions or for arriving late—which, according to God, might be on time—because they got lost on the way? No. "The LORD is gracious and compassionate, slow to anger and rich in love. The LORD is good to all; he has compassion on all he has made," the psalmist tells us (Psalm 145:8-9). The Lord is good to us. God is understanding and patient. It is often we who are exacting and impatient with ourselves. It is we who need to impart to ourselves the grace and mercy that God shows us and that we show others. Peace, my friend. Patience. "All shall be well," as Julian of Norwich said.[2]

So what can we know about the particularities of God's will for our lives? We can know this: *God leads us by our loves and desires*—our natural proclivities. Our joys.

But perhaps we do not know what we love or desire. We are not sure what brings us joy. Well, then, we need to seriously heed the words of author and activist Parker Palmer and "listen to our lives."[3]

That said, it is hard to follow Jesus and listen to our lives when we have too much stuff and when we have stuffed too many activities into our lives because we are shackled to societal markers of success, status, and comfort. In other words, the cares of this world (Matthew 13:22). And so we have to repent—to throw the extra stuff overboard (give it away) and simplify so that we have margin to hear and know God, to listen to our lives. And we don't listen to our lives alone; we do so with others.

I have often talked to my baby brother, Kenny, about his love for Case New Holland (CNH) tractors. He thinks about them all the time. "They build them tough," he says. "They're an example of good American engineering. I have been praying for years that the Italians who own CNH would sell the company back to an American owner because most of the big tractors are designed and made here in America."

My brother Kenny (who, by the way, is known as "Ken" to everyone else now that he is grown) once reminisced to

*So what can we know
about the particularities
of God's will for our lives?
We can know this:* God
leads us by our loves and
desires—*our natural
proclivities. Our joys.*

me about tractors. "Back in the day, each tractor was made differently. Every manufacturer did their own thing. Back then, tractors were not mass-produced." Recently he purchased a CNH from his sister-in-law to plow snow, cut wood, and move dirt. "I like to know how they run," he told me. Kenny has always loved tractors, but he got his undergraduate degree in business. I wasn't sure why. I told him, "Kenny, you ain't no office guy. You like to be outside. You could be an engineer who works on tractors, but it isn't like you to spend your day inside. Though I could see you running a tractor business . . ."

But Kenny likes to keep things interesting. About a decade ago, Kenny called me and asked me to pray that he could do a thousand sit-ups. He said, "I like challenging myself." He also asked me for years to pray that he would get into the Navy SEALs. He later started training with the Navy SEALs, but during that time he met Chelsea, his future wife, and decided not to pursue it after all. SEALs are away from home a lot and have an extremely high divorce rate. He wanted to be present with Chelsea and their future family.

Instead, Kenny trained to operate heavy equipment and become a John Deere mechanic. He needed to know how to operate heavy equipment to transport tractors and such. Besides, John Deere tractors are his second favorite after CNH. Kenny admitted that he had the interest and skill for the work.

Frankly, nothing about Kenny's life surprises me. He is my brother, and I have known him his whole life. He is being the person he has always been. As an adult, he is comfortable with being himself—with not wanting to be anyone else or compare himself to anyone else. I have not mentioned that Kenny also has pastoral gifts, has the gift of encouragement, knows Scripture, prays fervently, and has a good mind. He is without guile. Maybe one day he will be a bivocational pastor, given his spiritual gifts and abilities. Who knows?

As with Jesus, certain aspects of our callings are made manifest during different seasons of our lives. It is thought that Jesus was a carpenter for the first thirty or so years of his life, given that his earthly father, Joseph, was a carpenter. Then, after John the Baptist, Jesus' relative, baptized him in the Jordan River, he continued to follow his messianic call by ministering throughout Judea in the power of the Spirit while making his way to the Cross. This was the outworking of the Father's will for him. Like Jesus, my brother Kenny has pursued different callings in different seasons. Kenny is being led by his loves, desires, and joys. He told me, "I think to myself, *God could have made me any way he wanted to, but he chose to make me this way.*" Kenny is embracing who God is calling him to be in the world and not worrying about being someone else. He can't be.

Working with his hands, being outside, and doing any favor he can for others is how my brother bears Jesus as he journeys out on the seas of life. Kenny and his wife, Chelsea, are among the most generous people I have ever met—and they happen to be family. I can tell you this: I have never prayed to the Lord asking for anything related to CNH for myself. I have never dreamed about or wanted to do a thousand sit-ups. At no time have I wanted to be a Navy SEAL. My husband and I do not own tractors, nor do we see a need to. But thanks to Kenny, if I happen to see a tractor coming down the road or in a field, I can tell its make.

Embracing who we are and using our God-given gifts is a lesson we relearn throughout our lifetimes. It is part of embracing God's calling to set out to sea. Not knowing ourselves, or trying to be who we are not, will send us off course.

LED BY OUR PLACE

To the preacher who kept saying, "We must put God in our lives," the
Master said, "God is already there. Our business is to recognize this."

ANTHONY DE MELLO, SJ

OUR SPIRITUAL FORMATION, which allows us to journey deeper into the life of God and further into the Kingdom, happens in a particular place: right here in these circumstances. This location. These waters. Not over there, where we assume things would be smooth sailing. God is right here in the boat with us.

Guidance in Difficult Places

"But I don't want to be here" or "I am tired of being here. It is so hard," we say sometimes. However, difficulty *right here* is not an automatic excuse to move to *over there*.

Years ago, I was employed at a Christian organization that

had a large population of people who had a limited view of the gospel's effects. They took umbrage with me because I believe one way the American church can usher in shalom is by casting Jesus' life preservers out to our neighbors caught in the deadly seas of our US immigration system, where the culture of death reigns supreme—stealing, killing, and destroying people every day. Drowning them. I am part of a coast guard fleet of Jesus boats patrolling these deadly immigration waters on behalf of the church. But it wasn't just immigration. The other employees resisted my posture toward alleviating poverty, addressing racism, and caring for creation. And I was resisting American Christians' participation in the creation of death worlds for all sorts of people. As C. S. Lewis famously wrote in *The Magician's Nephew*, "What you see and hear depends a good deal on where you are standing: it also depends on what sort of person you are."[1] These folks had not stood where I've stood or seen what I've seen. Erasing the need for abortion and maintaining religious freedom are not at odds with anything I was advocating for, like immigration reform and a broader safety net for the poor, which are needed because most of us as individuals and families do not give enough to sustain God's children in need.

I did not learn my beliefs from the Democratic party or from the Republican party. I learned them from reading the Bible for two to four hours a day as a young girl, from learning Christian history, and from being poor and living and working among the poor. At the organization I was working for at that time, I was careful to answer when asked about these realities, not to shove my opinion down anyone's throat. Yet I found myself living against the grain.

Commenting on the Desert Fathers' and Mothers' conviction that our lives are wrapped up with our neighbors' lives, theologian Rowan Williams writes, "Gaining the brother or sister and winning God are linked. . . . It is opening doors for them to healing and to wholeness. Insofar as you open such doors for another, you gain God, in the sense that you become a place where God happens for somebody else."[2] I just wanted the church to open doors for others—to be a place where God happens for those the church comes into contact with (especially the marginalized)—instead of throwing them overboard into the Mediterranean Sea to be eaten by sharks. Among the marginalized and poor in spirit has often been the place where God happens for me.

Meanwhile, my husband and I knew beyond a shadow of a doubt that we were called to that place. Our assurance never wavered. But what a place it was! It could often be sandpaper to my nerves, friction to my soul. Downright excruciating. Jesus and I were sailing rough seas. *I am tired of going against the grain, Lord. Why did you put us here?* I asked repeatedly. *This is an outpost—way out. It would be so much easier if we were assigned to _____. How come other people I know get to be there? They are living the life while we have to put up with this.* After some weeks of grumbling, the Lord spoke to me. I remember it as clear as day, though it was late on a Friday night. I had been in our bedroom, about to cross the threshold into the hall when the Lord caught me off guard and said, *You know why you are here? Because the people here would never dream of going to* _____. *So I am bringing what they would learn at* _____ *to them through you and Shawn.*

God also had plans to teach us and grow us while we were there. Some of the most beautiful, grace-filled people I have ever met were there, too, sailing along with us. Teaching us. Being there was crucial for my formation and for the trajectory of my life. I knew our being there was not a mistake. It was for a season. And although it ended up being one of the most painful seasons of our lives (as well as one of the most beautiful), I would not wish it away. I would not be here had I not gone there.

Indeed, God sometimes sends us on journeys to places that are not our first choice. Maybe they are even our last choice. We see no possibilities, no grace. Therefore, it is when we set sail with Jesus to such places that we are to keep watch for the glory of God, for grace, for rescues, for choirs of angels appearing to us in the night sky as we sail these rough and sometimes lonely seas in obedience. We will not be stuck forever in chaos with Jesus in the boat. Still, we have to learn and relearn that it is here, in the places God leads us, that we will experience the glory of God.

Guidance out of Death-Dealing Places

There is a difference between difficult and death-dealing. We should feel free to shake the dust off our sandals and bid

*We will not be stuck
forever in chaos with Jesus
in the boat. Still, we have
to learn and relearn that
it is here, in the places
God leads us, that we
will experience the glory
of God.*

a place *adios*, leaving it in the hands of God, when we find ourselves in toxic and abusive situations. There can come a moment when we cannot do and be anymore because we are not received. Shawn, I, and others were forced to leave the place of which I spoke when it went from difficult to poisonous. There are "Christian" environments—churches, organizations, relationships, and workplaces—that are far more destructive to our souls than "secular" environments would be. So we ought to feel free to flee, to sail to a port of refuge, though this will likely take preparation and planning before we set out.

But maybe we feel stuck in such a situation. Maybe it is a work environment, and we are in desperate need of the paycheck it provides. Or maybe we are apprehensive and fearful about ending a relationship because at least its toxicity and abuse are familiar—a familiar sort of death, that is—and we are too scared to set sail into life unknown. This is nothing to take lightly; there could be a real fallout as we flee for our lives—financial, emotional, physical, spiritual, relational, and otherwise. In these situations, healing can only come through leaving. Seldom do toxic environments, systems, or relationships change. If they do, it can take years; meanwhile people will suffer the consequences.

It is not God's will that you be abused or remain in abuse, whether the abuse is emotional, spiritual, physical, financial, verbal, or sexual. That's not the place for you. That is not the place of Jesus; it's the place of demons and the devil, who steal, kill, and destroy (John 10:10). Do not let false guilt or lies keep you from leaving. God is not a gaslighter. Some people may be, but God is not. You will likely need help getting out. Do not hesitate to ask trustworthy people for help. Sadly, trustworthy souls may not be leaders or people in your Christian community. Find such folks wherever you can, particularly among trained professionals.

Joseph, Mary, and the baby Jesus did not wait around for King Herod to kill them. They fled to seek refuge in Egypt. In fact, it was an angel of the Lord who told them to get out (Matthew 2:13). Interestingly enough, the angel did *not* tell them that it was God's will for them to stay there and take abuse from Herod. If you are reading this and sensing that you need to get out of an abusive relationship, well, then consider me your angel telling you to escape. Paul once escaped in a basket that his friends lowered down from Damascus's city wall to save his life (Acts 9:23-25). There are many examples in Scripture of people fleeing violence and abuse.

If healing requires leaving, we may need a break from a certain church or Christian community we have known because it has rammed our boat and nearly destroyed us. This kind of place may not be an ark of salvation or a place of recovery. Deep wounds require rehabilitation and time to heal. Some of us need to be rebuilt because we have merely a skeleton of a boat left with which to bear Jesus. And God provides for us in our convalescence. Think about how he sent an angel to feed Elijah in the wilderness when Elijah fled after Jezebel threatened his life (1 Kings 19:1-9) and angels to minister to Jesus after the devil tempted him (Matthew 4:11).

This is God's heart for us, so unlike the ramming of our boats by some "Christian" communities.

Where do we belong? Where we are known and loved. Appreciated. Where we see and are seen. Where our absence is noticed and our presence cherished. Of course we are known, loved, and cherished by God. But much of the time God reveals his love for us through others. We know Jesus prepares a place for us with him at the end of our age. Can we trust that he prepares places for us here just as we ought to prepare a refreshing place for him to rest inside us—in our boat?

God's Will: Loving Our Religiopolitical Enemies in Place

I am very close with my sister, Michelle; brother Marco; sister-in-law Shelly; brother Kenny; sister-in-law Chelsea; and dad. I would live on the same plot of land—yea, even far removed from much of civilization—with them in a heartbeat if Shawn and I could find jobs as professors in their area. But alas, we cannot.

But it would be a mistake to assume that Shawn and I and my family members are so close because we are politically and denominationally homogeneous. We are not. We often disagree vehemently about politics. Even so, politics is not worth a familial divorce, though familial divorce and divorce among friends is widespread in our culture these days. We are becoming more and more separated from God and one another. Is that not also a form of hell? I do not know if these are the "last days," but these words of Jesus often haunt me: "At that time many will turn away from the faith and will betray and hate each other. . . . Because of the increase of wickedness, *the love of most will grow cold*" (Matthew 24:10, 12, emphasis added).

Any one of my family members whom I consider political "Samaritans" (and vice versa) would stop on the road to Jericho to attend to the wounds of their political and ideological foes should they come upon them. They would not cross to the other side pretending they didn't see them or refuse to stop because the person was "an enemy." They would give the person the shirt off their back and put them up in their own home or a hotel without asking for anything in return. No doubt they would follow up months or even years later to make sure the person was flourishing. I'm sure of this, even though my dad calls me weekly to jokingly harass me about every political upheaval and tell me that my position is untenable.

I have spoken and written repeatedly about how Jesus' own disciples were probably political enemies with one another. Among his followers were a radical Zealot who wanted to violently take down Rome, those originally in cahoots with Rome (like Matthew), monastic Essenes, rural Galileans considered backward troublemakers, former Pharisees, and so on. Yet they each had a place in the heart of Jesus and the hearts of one another. Even Judas did until he chose to leave his place of kinship and belovedness seemingly because Jesus was not riding the wave of his religio-socio-political

BEARING GOD

popularity to deliver them from Roman occupation (at least not in the way that Judas thought he should).

We see that Jesus made the reality of his political posture public when he answered Pilate's interrogation with this statement: "My kingdom is not of this world. If it were, my servants would fight to prevent my arrest by the Jewish leaders. But now my kingdom is from another place" (John 18:36). Jesus' refusal to violently overthrow the government seemed to play a role in the crowd asking Pilate to release Barabbas instead of him. After all, it was Barabbas, not Jesus, who had taken part in a political uprising against Rome (John 18:40). Barabbas could be counted on to do what it took, to die, for the good of his country. Jesus could not. He would not. At least not in the way the crowd imagined. So they sentenced him to death.

Maybe we can't imagine ourselves sentencing our political foes to death. Oh, but we could. If we elevate politics over following Jesus, finding a sort of salvation in our allegiance to a particular political party, I am not so sure that we wouldn't put people to death when passionately inflamed. Concerning such places where there is an "illusion of separateness," Father Gregory Boyle writes, "It is in this place where we judge the other and feel the impossibility of anything getting bridged. The gulf too wide and the gap too distant, the walls grow higher, and we forget who we are meant to be to each other."[3]

Jesus transcends gaps. Narrows them. Knocks down walls of separation and reminds us of who we are meant to be to each other. He loved Judas. Broke bread with Judas. Confided

40

in Judas. But in the garden of Gethsemane, it was Judas who broke confidence, who did not love Jesus (if love is understood to be seeking the good of another). It was Judas who widened the gap and erected a wall of separation between them. We may not like our political or even theological foes, but we do have to love them, which may require more of us than liking them would. That is the miracle of Christ's life in us. In the words of Father Boyle, when we live in such a way, "we have a chance, sometimes, to create a new jurisdiction, a place of astonishing mutuality, whenever we close both eyes of judgment and open the other eye to pay attention. Reminding each other how acceptable we are. . . . Suddenly, we find ourselves in the same room with each other and the walls are gone."[4]

So one thing we have to do in our local places and spheres of influence is love our religiopolitical enemies instead of demonize them. Dismantle walls of separation. "We seek to create loving communities of kinship precisely to counteract mounting lovelessness, racism, and the cultural disparagement that keeps us apart," notes Boyle.[5] You and I are to "bring heaven to earth," as my friend Carl says, as best as we can, wherever we find ourselves. After all, are we not bearing Jesus in us, the Jesus who loved Judas, the God who is even good to the wicked and ungrateful? If we do not come bearing Christ and his gifts to whomever we encounter because we have thrown Christ overboard in order to get what we want or what we think he wants, we are not following Jesus. Of all people, we Christians ought to be defined by our love for enemies and by the way we leave the world better than we found it.

Our Place

It is of great import that we be very deliberate about the Christian communities we attach ourselves to, because these communities will influence our formation (or malformation), our ability to discern the will of God, and the decisions we make. They influence what we do, know, and become—our lives. We cannot escape the influence of the culture in which each of us resides. It is discipling us for good or for ill or for mediocrity. Our places either awaken us to participate in life, anesthetize us to life, or train us to produce and participate in a culture of death.

Not long ago, I was talking to my best friend, Debora, about how important it is that I be truly known and loved in my church community. For a short while, when the pandemic restrictions lifted, Shawn and I attended a new church. I pointed the Jesus boat in a different direction. It's not because there was anything wrong with the church we belonged to; on the contrary, we loved it. The church we belonged to was only three miles away but in another town and school system. I was trying to hold true to my ideal of being part of a church in my immediate community, a parish church (and perhaps more liturgical one) within the boundary lines of my town. So I thought, *Maybe we ought to change churches.* Mami had just died, and I thought I should return

Of all people, we Christians ought to be defined by our love for enemies and by the way we leave the world better than we found it.

to the church of our roots. I could feel close to her there. Maybe it was where I was supposed to be.

We ended up attending the new church for about six months. It had a wonderful liturgy, but I found it difficult to get to know people during a pandemic, even though the pandemic was slowing. I believe the lack of communion we experienced was partly due to the fact that we were wearing masks—a necessary and good public-health measure—and partly because no one could invite another over in good conscience. Moreover, the church was so big that we were anonymous in a sea of faces. No one knew me or my family. They could not appreciate the gifts we bore forth.

In my phone conversation with Debora, it occurred to me just how important it is to be known: "God forbid, if Shawn or I were to get sick, or something were to happen to one of our daughters, I would want to be among pastors and church members who knew and cared about us." Then it struck me: "Why are we leaving our good and healthy church for some ideal? Our church is three miles away. They love us. They know us. They care for us." It is such a grace, so comforting, to have pastoral pastors who have known my family for years. Who love my daughters. Who love Shawn. Pastor Joanie visited Mami in a local hospital when Shawn and I were away for our anniversary and she and my dad were watching the girls. Pastor Russ showed up when Iliana was eight years old (she is now fifteen) when she had her tonsils and adenoids removed and awoke from surgery disoriented. At the time, doctors thought she might have hemophilia, so a routine tonsillectomy and adenoidectomy were not routine for her. Pastor Russ was concerned about her and about me and Shawn. Pastor Russ and Pastor Joanie's presence throughout the ordeal meant so much to us.

When we had been new in our previous town, Christians down the street we'd just met, Emily and Ben, had watched our daughters Iliana and Valentina when Isabella was born. When our little Iz was diagnosed as "failure to thrive," Pastor Larry; his wife, Marti; and other members of St. Andrews came to the hospital repeatedly. (Thank God Isabella is thriving now as a free-spirited firecracker.) Pastor Barry, appointed to our current church after Pastor Russ retired, visited us to introduce himself, in our yard, while the pandemic raged. We liked him right away. All throughout my life, my pastors have known and loved me. From Pastor Boyce at our little country church when I was a child to Pastor Bob and his wife, Jan, who would come at the drop of a hat should there be an emergency even though they lived three hours away. My daughters have a history with our pastors and communities. It is good to be around long enough to have a history with people.

Never underestimate the availability of community members to be present in the mundane or in time of need. In a modern, transient world of seemingly ubiquitous alienation, where each home seems to be its own island, it means the world when our pastors and church members and others in the body of Christ care for me and my family when hurricanes storm into our lives. They are lighthouses lighting the way, beacons in the night, and the coast guard, offering to rescue us and tow us back to shore when we are in great peril. They have saved our lives too many times to count.

We returned to the church we love. It was right where we were supposed to be all along. Even though it is technically in another town, it's not too far away for us to love and be loved. The church members are helping me become who I am.

Our Calling to Community in Place

It is in the context of healthy community and relationships that we find ourselves. It is in looking into the eyes of God and seeing delight and in looking into the eyes of those who seek our good and who delight in us that we see ourselves reflected. God and others who love us name and draw out the good in us. They see good things we do not see or acknowledge about ourselves. They help us discern next steps. Discernment does not happen when we are alone or in a vacuum, for we do not live for ourselves alone. Discernment happens in context. It happens in place.

Rampant American individualism, where the self is elevated above all, is a rip-off. A counterfeit. The myth of individualism, that *Invictus-ing*, is an existential lie. We cannot live alone and isolated, though it is the way of Western, American culture. In large cities and churches, we can disappear. The same is also happening more and more in small towns because of technology gone too far. It is invasive and isolating. In such circumstances, nothing is asked of us.

Nothing is required of us, and we can coast by in anonymity if we choose. During the Industrial Revolution, people fled small towns for the cities not only in search of work but also in search of anonymity. A few generations later, we are wrecked by that anonymity, which has led to a terrorizing epidemic of loneliness. We are alienated from God and one another, but our lives, churches, and communities are meant to embody the spirit of the old television show *Cheers*—where everybody knows our names and is always glad we came, no matter who we are.[6] Most of Paul's New Testament letters weren't addressed to individuals. They were addressed to churches in certain cities or regions. No one is a self-made person. We stand on the shoulders of and are influenced by others. So whenever you hear "He is a self-made man" or "She did everything herself," you can let that falsehood sail right on by. It's never true.

But what *is* true is that our alienation from God and one another is hell on earth. It produces weeping and gnashing of teeth. Anxiety. Loneliness. We are made in the image of God, and God is not isolated. Perhaps that is why God said that it's not good for humans to be alone (Genesis 2:18). God—Father, Son, and Holy Spirit—is not alone. We cannot face the vast ocean—life—alone. We depend on God and one another to make it to our destination. Indigenous peoples, people in the Majority World, and the wise of all sorts know this to be true: We depend on one another and creation. Whoever we are and whatever we do affects others, for good or for ill. As I have written elsewhere, Jesus depended on the nourishment and presence of his mother and on the presence, companionship, and comfort of his disciples.[7] Leave us alone and isolated too long and we conjure up delusions about reality, narratives that do not exist. Without healthy people to counteract our delusions, illusions, tunnel vision, and fantasies, we run aground. Others in our place, and even some from afar, play a part in our conversions to following Christ. There are always parts of us that need to be converted to following Jesus. We are not yet wholly made new (Revelation 21:5).

Consequently, being deliberate about our place—where we live and whom we are surrounded by—is of great import. What I mean is that it's not always wise to take the higher-paying job away from family, friends, and other members of your Christian community. Strangely enough, it is counter-cultural, even in the American church, to keep money from making our decisions. Money is not a good god. But good relationships are priceless. Making a lot of money and having the finest houses should never be the determining factor for the direction of our lives, for our place. We should consider other things. What will happen if we get sick? Who is going to take care of us in places where we are unknown? Who will be there to rejoice with us when good things happen? Who will give us wise counsel? Who will marry us and bury us? Who and what communities are, have been, or will be Christ to us?

5

LED BY DISCERNMENT

In the silence of the heart God speaks. . . .
Listening is the beginning of prayer.

MOTHER TERESA

WHAT IF YOU HAVE A DECISION TO MAKE and you don't know what to do? You have no map or clear navigation instructions. And you can't keep doing what you are doing. You have to change. You have to do something. The time has come. Not deciding is deciding (ultimately, to keep things as they are currently). That is not an option.

Fortunately, we are not bereft of wisdom for uncharted waters. The Lord does not leave us floating aimlessly at sea, just to be tossed this way and that. We might not always know what is going on, but Jesus in us is directing us if we are obeying him the best we know how and listening. Again, God is not standing around waiting to swat us down like we would swat at annoying flies or mosquitoes buzzing around in our homes. God is always for us. Always. He is never against us. We might travel our own way and destroy ourselves and bring harm to others because we have free will. This is not of God. This is of ourselves and the devil and his demons. But if we are saying yes to God, we have help discerning what to do.

The following practices, though not exhaustive, can help us discern God's will. Perhaps certain practices will be more helpful for us in one season than another, depending on the circumstances.

Listening

Is there a restlessness in your soul? Something not sitting right? An emptiness? A recurring desire that will not leave you alone? Perhaps you feel God calling you to a new path but can't quite put your finger on what it is.

No doubt the amount of external noise in our world frays our nerves. It makes us unwell. Militaries throughout the world use incessant noise, even music, to torture prisoners.[1] We were not meant to live loud, to metaphorically have background music constantly playing like it does in American restaurants and stores (and now even while we are pumping gas). It is torture to the soul. Makes for bad decisions.[2] Contributes to depression and anxiety.[3] Drowns out and distracts us from the voice of God, from wisdom. We can only hear clearly from God when we are in stillness, solitude, and quiet. Jesus frequently got away to places like the mountains or the desert or the Sea of Galilee or the garden of Gethsemane to pray, to have silence and solitude, to seek the will of the Father.

I'll never forget what an Anglican bishop once said to a group at a summer conference at Duke Divinity School: "You all are always inside. In the air-conditioning. In front of computer screens. How can you do theology? How can you hear God if you are never out in his creation? How can you hear God if you are never silent?" His words hung suspended in the air. What could we say? Outside is good for us. He was right. So, then, what do we do? We mute or say goodbye to social media and that which keeps us from listening. We do what we can to spend time in nature. Solitude and quiet allow us to pay attention to our lives and to what God is saying. These things are necessary for discernment and growth.

And we must listen to our bodies. Does the thought of our current situation, a relationship, or an opportunity bring us anxiety? Are we angry, depressed, or constantly miserable at the thought of these things? Are we burned out or stressed out? Our bodies are trying to tell us something. Our bodies speak. A clue from your body doesn't automatically mean that something isn't God's will—because that could be the effects of trauma speaking in a healthy situation—but if we are experiencing negative feelings in our bodies, we can be sure that something is not right. There is something we need to address. We can go to God and to wise people for guidance. They could be trained and credentialed therapists, spiritual directors, friends, pastors, or all of them!

God's Pace

Achievement and notoriety don't fill us. The hidden secret of life that so many are looking for is not secret. It is in the stability and simple rhythms that keep us in God, with each other, and in wholeness.

The rat race and fast pace of this American life and church subculture has me frazzled. It is inhumane. Add sickness, Mami's death, the deaths of others due to COVID-19 and police brutality, our death politics, school pressures, financial insecurity, the needs of my family, hatred in the world—it's no wonder I am tired. This inhumanity has bled into the church. For a moment in time, at the beginning of the pandemic, we were forced to slow down. To savor our time together when we had no other options but to do so. This was before employers figured out that they could demand more hours of our days because we were working from home. The public sphere has invaded the private. It seeks to own us.

The pace at which we constantly function militates against our ability to sit and savor our lives and the lives of those around us. To be still. It's not surprising that many Americans accept the Christian and work rat race as normal. Even so, it is not healthy. I, too, must take responsibility for giving in to a culture that pushes me to function beyond what human nature prescribes. When I pause, it is as if I am sitting by watching everything happen, the way I sit on my porch and watch cars whiz by well above the posted speed limit with no wherewithal to slow them down. This pace through time and space, coupled with the fracturing of communities and relationships, is killing us.

We tend to think we are free here in America —"land of the free and home of the brave" and all that.[4] But if we are truly free, why are we nearly dead? Our supposed freedom has not given us life; instead, we find ourselves blanketed with ubiquitous gun violence, depression, loneliness, and despair. This famous line from the movie *Fight Club* perfectly describes the current zeitgeist:

> Man, I see in Fight Club the strongest and smartest men who've ever lived. I see all this potential, and I see squandering. . . . An entire generation pumping gas, waiting tables; slaves with white collars. Advertising has us chasing cars and clothes, working jobs we hate so we can buy [stuff] we don't need. We're the middle children of history, man. No purpose or place. We have no Great War. No Great Depression. Our Great War's a spiritual war. Our Great Depression is our lives. We've all been raised on television to believe that one day we'd all be millionaires, and movie gods, and rock stars. But we won't. And we're slowly learning that fact. And we're very, very pissed off.[5]

Indeed, we are in one of the richest countries in the world, but we are miserable. Our success and the supposed pace necessary for it does not produce happiness and peace. Stability.

In order for us to survive and thrive, many things have to

go overboard, including our breakneck speed of life. A broken neck does not serve us well. For healing, get rid of that which does not matter. Not only is it good to declutter our homes; it is also good to declutter our lives and schedules so that we and others may truly live. When I think about famous musicians who have lost their lives to suicide, I think about the philosopher in the book of Ecclesiastes. He, too, had almost everything a person could ever want and lived a culturally fast life. After sizing everything up and exploring the meaning of life, he concluded with this simple yet profound statement: "Now all has been heard; here is the conclusion of the matter: Fear God and keep his commandments, for this is the duty of all mankind. For God will bring every deed into judgment, including every hidden thing, whether it is good or evil" (Ecclesiastes 12:13-14). Neither the riches nor the fast pace fulfills us. Knowing and obeying God does—because in the end we will all be judged.

Way Open

Parker Palmer talks about the "way open."[6] I like that terminology, so I will use the phrase here to describe making seemingly effortless headway on our sea voyage even if we cannot tell exactly where we are going. When we are thinking about discerning God's will for the next step of our lives, let us consider whether the path is opening before us. Is the "way open"? This doesn't mean that what we're called to do does not require effort or that there is no difficulty involved;

our callings are always tested in this world the way Jesus' was in the wilderness (Matthew 4:1-11). But the question here is whether our next step is unobstructed.

For me, this journey most recently started when a friend called me last summer to tell me a faculty position at a seminary was open and encouraged me to apply. I objected. "I won't have my PhD in hand in time for the start of the position," I said. But I ended up applying anyway.

A few weeks later, someone told me about a local faculty position that had recently become available. The job ad said they would consider someone close to finishing their PhD. But I knew that there were many qualified people with their PhDs who would apply to both jobs. Such positions seldom come open. When I heard about it, I was like, *Lord, why are two seemingly ideal positions in my area of expertise coming open before I am finished with my PhD? They are the best chances I have for getting a job as a professor, but the timing is off. Lord, are you punking me?* I obviously knew the Lord wasn't "punking" me, but it seemed uncanny that the two positions I hoped for opened up at the same time and before I was finished with my degree! I thought that was cruel timing even though I know God is not cruel. God is for me.

Northeastern Seminary called me for a virtual interview. I made it through that hoop. Then they flew me out for an on-campus interview. Early the morning before the interview I said to the Lord, *Why am I here? Why am I even doing this interview? There is no way this is going to work out. Shawn and I can't live seven hours apart to follow our*

When we are thinking about discerning God's will for the next step of our lives, let us consider whether the path is opening before us.

callings as professors. We don't want to tear our family apart.
He has a good job and is almost a full professor. You know that
for him to leave his teaching position so I can take this one if
it is offered to me is career suicide from a human standpoint.
Then I said, *Please make me not like it here. Don't do this to*
me. It's a waste of time and money for me to be here if nothing
is going to come of it. It would be driving a sword through my
heart if I love it and then have to turn it down should it be
offered to me.

I interviewed all day. I treasured my interactions with
faculty, staff, and students. I was most nervous about my
teaching demonstration, even though I have been teaching
seminary classes as an adjunct professor for years and got
rave reviews from undergraduate students at my doctoral
institution. But several Northeastern students told me that I
"knocked it out of the park." Throughout the day I felt like I
was in my zone, like I was made to teach spiritual formation
at a seminary level.

That night I called Shawn and said, "I loved it! I really
want this job but cannot see how it is going to work out.
Should I just withdraw my candidacy?" Shawn said that that
was a bad idea. After thinking about it, I thought withdraw-
ing was a bad idea too. Why close the door on myself when
I would love the job? It would be a different thing altogether
if I hated it or had doubts about it. No, I would wait for God
to close it for me.

The next week, I was interviewed virtually for the second
position (the local one). I told Shawn, "The worst outcome

for our family would be a double jeopardy where I get neither of the positions." He agreed. It's hard to live on one full salary and a graduate stipend—we need two reasonable incomes. It turned out I had to wait several weeks to hear from Northeastern Seminary. Regarding the second position, it seemed to be the obvious choice for me since it was local.

So far, the way seemed open for both positions. Palmer notes that a standard word of counsel from the Quakers that is useful for us all is to be patient and "have faith" because the "way will open"—eventually.[7] Waiting is key, but none of us like to do it. It can be excruciating. I had to wait for over a decade, preparing myself in the meantime, to get to the point where I qualified for a full-time job as a seminary professor. The way was not open a decade ago.

Way Closed

Sometimes the way closes. Palmer writes about a time when he was extremely frustrated because no way was opening for him. He did everything he could think of to discern his calling but came up empty-handed. In exasperation, he sought the counsel of a wise Quaker named Ruth. He told Ruth of his woes and how seemingly every attempt he made to move forward in his vocational call had been stymied. This was Ruth's response: "In sixty-plus years of living, way has never opened in front of me. . . . But a lot of way has closed behind me, and that's had the same guiding effect."[8] Palmer observes how he learned a great life lesson that day: "There is as much guidance in what does not and cannot happen in my life as there is in what can and does—maybe more."[9]

I was waiting to hear from Northeastern when I found out that I did not make it to the second round of interviews for the local position. I was devastated, even though it was a clear answer. I had asked God to shut the door if it was not to be. The gut punch came because I'd thought I had a shot at it and because it made the most practical sense for my family's current situation. I knew some people at the school, the girls could stay at their schools, and we would not have to relocate away from Shawn's mom and brother and his family. However, the way closed for the commonsense option. But shortly after, I was over the moon when Northeastern Seminary offered me the position of Assistant Professor of Spiritual Formation. We will be moving to Rochester, New York, within a year of this writing.

Fear

We cannot give in to fear or allow fear to control our decisions. Before Northeastern offered me the job, I asked Shawn if I should take it if it were offered to me. "Marlena," he said, "that job is a perfect fit for you, and the environment is perfect for you. I could not think of a better position for you." "I know," I said. "But what about you? What if your university does not work with you to let you do the work remotely? You're almost a full professor. Chair of the department. I don't want you to have to start over on the bottom rung of tenure track. You have worked too hard and too long for that."

As I write, we are in the in-between space, waiting on God to see what will happen with Shawn's position. How will Jesus prepare a place for him as we journey together in faith? I don't know at this moment. But both of us, and those closest to us, are convinced that God has led me to Northeastern and our family to Rochester. We know and are loved by people there, we love the seminary, and we feel like it is home even though we have not lived in the area for fifteen years.

God often asks us to move past our fear to obey him. And as I have said many times before to my undergraduate and seminary students, for some people, waking up and getting out of bed, putting one foot in front of the other, is the most courageous thing they can do each day. And that is God's call for them today. For us, it is moving without yet knowing Shawn's place. "If it doesn't take courage to do what you are doing, then maybe you're not doing all that God has invited you to do," my friend Debora once said. I think she is on to something.

Values

What do we value? As far as my natural bents go, I teach, preach, offer pastoral care, and write. I value all those things. At times, I organize and lead initiatives to reform the US immigration system and help those who have been caught in the immigration death world the US has created. I work alongside migrant workers who harvest the produce and meat we eat here in America. I see how they are oppressed and mistreated. I value people over profit. That is why, for example, I would never work for a company that values profit over people and mistreats its workers.

Since college, given my penchant for American and church history, spiritual formation, and practical theology, I have become intimately acquainted with the history of racism in the US and the myriad of ways that racism continues to manifest itself here at the hands of professing Christians. Because of racism and greed, we stole Native American lands and embraced the institution of slavery. These harsh realities—and God's call for us to seek justice (Isaiah 1:17; Micah 6:8)—are why I work to expose personal and systemic racism in my generation.

I must be in nature frequently. I suppose that's why I abhor the pollution and poisoning of the earth. I recycle as much as I can and try not to buy clothes often. I give them away when I am done with them and recycle those that cannot be given away. Sometimes I borrow clothes from my two oldest daughters, Iliana and Valentina. I really do not like to buy stuff we don't need, but that's hard because my children like knickknacks. Moreover, I cannot be Scrooge-like and forbid my children from having any toys.

I also value my family, my parents, my siblings, and their families. I try to spend as much time as I can with them. I value time, and I know that it is short. I value people over money too. Most of all, I hope that I value God above all because God truly is my life.

Think about what you value and how it influences the trajectory of your life and the decisions you make. Live according to your values and conscience, and you will be doing, knowing, and being the person you are meant to be in the world. We will have to reevaluate and reprioritize throughout our lives so that we do not chase after other gods. Let us not sell our souls by attaching undue significance to things that do not matter.

A qualification is in order here. Those with corrupted spirits who are following the way of wickedness might live in accordance with their corrupted values and their corrupted consciences. The Ku Klux Klan does. Hitler did. These are salient examples. All those who operate out of corruption and any kind of evil are not being who God meant them to be in the world. We cannot become who we are meant to be if we go against the way of Jesus—the path of truth, love, justice, wisdom, and holiness—in little or big ways.

Affirmations

No one has ever told me that I would make a fantastic certified public accountant or Olympian. No one. But I have been told I am pastoral and prophetic. "The best professor I have ever had. Encouraging. Discerning. Brave. Peaceful," a student wrote. I have also heard, "That talk was amazing. Convicting. You're such a good preacher." And I've been told that I can say hard things nicely—that I offer a "spoonful of sugar [that] helps the medicine go down."[10] Shawn has repeatedly said, "I would never get away with saying that to students. They would detest me, but they still love you."

How have people affirmed you? Although you might downplay compliments in the moment, think about what people have said to you over the years. Think about the positive things that those who love you and care about you have said. Those are clues to your calling, abilities, and the general trajectory of God's will for your life.

We need not try to live out of our weaknesses. If I hate accounting and do not have the ability to do it, it's not for me. If I loathe my accounting job yet have extraordinary accounting ability, it does not necessarily mean that I must continue in that direction. There are things I have an ability to do, a knack for, and an enjoyment of but that are not necessarily God's will for my life or place for me now.

The same is true for you—God isn't asking you to live out of your weaknesses. And even if you enjoy doing something but don't see a way to do more of it right now, that doesn't mean that it isn't part of God's will for your life in the future. Maybe you started out liking whatever it is you're doing currently but are sensing that it's almost time for a change. If you are unsure about which direction to go, think about what people have affirmed in your life.

Relationships

I do not have any toxic people in my inner circle. I am very careful about who has access to me. I only share myself with trustworthy people. If you sense that someone is not trust-worthy or reliable, do not entrust yourself to them. Moreover, if someone has shown themselves to be a snake, do not expect them to act otherwise. That is foolishness; they will take you down with them.

We have to do the work to disentangle ourselves from bad relationships. And we need to pay attention to red flags in relationships when we sense them. I have at times gaslit myself about the red flags I've seen, telling myself that I'm making something out of nothing. Sometimes I've mentioned those signs to another person and they've dismissed my concerns but then it's turned out that I was right. Some have said that I have the gift of discernment of spirits. Perhaps I do. Even if discerning others' true character doesn't come naturally to you, it's important that you're careful about whom you are in any kind of relationship with.

It is good to surround ourselves with people we admire and seek to be like—people who are what Jesus called "the salt of the earth" (Matthew 5:13). They do not have to be like us at all, but they should be full of goodness and seek the flourishing of others. In fact, we should *seek* to know healthy people who are different from us. They will expand our sou' and show us more of the beauty, truth, goodness, and ^{le}

in the world. They will rub off on us and vice versa. Truly, relationships can make or break us.

Ignatian Discernment

Saint Ignatius of Loyola, a sixteenth-century priest and theologian, has some lessons for us on discernment. I cannot list them all here but will list a few (and want to note that these types of discernment are practiced in healthy community). A fairly straightforward Ignatian discernment practice is to list the pros and cons of making a particular decision and weigh them. If the pros are weightier, then go in that direction.

Another method of Ignatian discernment is to consider whether the thought of something arouses desolation (negative feelings and unease) or consolation (comfort and a yes in our spirits) in us. Consolation is a sort of reassurance that what we're contemplating doing is right; desolation suggests the opposite.

My friend Debora, who is a spiritual director, has said that the concept of "sponge and rock" works best for her. When we consider something, do we sponge it up, easily absorbing it? That is consolation. Or does it hit our souls like water on a rock, running right off? If the latter, that is a no. Desolation.

Opportunities

Just because an opportunity comes up does not mean you have to take it. Be silent, pray, and seek counsel about opportunities that present themselves to you, whether they relate to vocation, calling, place, or relationships. If there is not an immediate yes in your spirit or if you sense an immediate no in your spirit, pay attention.

This might sound like trite advice, but here is why it is not. In some Christian circles, people have been taught to outright distrust their inclinations because "the heart is deceitful above all things and beyond cure" (Jeremiah 17:9). Of course, there is a legitimate sense in which we cannot trust ourselves to always do what is right. But acknowledging that truth is a far cry from being convinced that oneself and one's inclinations are bitter enemies to be disregarded and despised. If we are emotionally healthy, abiding in Christ, not knowingly disobeying God, and seeking his will within a trusted circle of wise and godly people who will gently question us if they see that something is off, we can trust our instincts. If there is a no, is it because of fear or prejudice, or is it born of wisdom? If we are unsure, we can convene what the Quakers call a "clearness committee." This means asking trusted people to listen to us and discern with us what they hear God saying in the situation. I have been asked to be a part of clearness committees and have asked others to be in such groups for me. It has been helpful—because, again, we do not live our lives alone.

However, if you are sensing that you are moving in a new direction, keep your eyes peeled for opportunities. As you patiently wait, you will find them in the most interesting of places. God will work with you through his Word, the ancient wisdom of the faith, and the guidance of others to help you go in the direction he has for you.

Do What You Want

Perhaps we have tried all these methods of discernment and nothing has been revealed to us, so we are at a crossroads. Well, there is a school of thought that says, "Love God, love your neighbor, and do what you want—as long as it is out of an expression of love for God and neighbor." I believe this is good. If we are loving God and our neighbors and then paying attention to what our lives are saying, our bents and proclivities, the affirmations we have received, and the ways that are opening, *then* we should do what we want. We must make the best decision we can. As Shawn says, "Live out of love without freaking out, without tearing your hair out wondering *Should I be doing this?* because you are not 100 percent sure."

Storms

Embracing God's will for our lives, going out to sea, means that we will not always have smooth sailing. Storms can come when we least expect them. Sometimes we can see storms approaching, but often they are either not as bad as we anticipate or worse than we ever imagined. The only thing we can do in storms is try to survive them with the help of others, trusting that Christ, whom we bear, will get us through them eventually. And if we can't trust, we can have others pray for us and trust for us. Tow us.

There's no need to berate ourselves because we are not doing this or that or because we are not moving along at the speed we would like. No need to berate ourselves because we can't see where we are going. It is hard to see in storms. Sometimes it's downright impossible. So we hold on for dear life to Jesus in us. We issue distress calls—call for help when we need it. We put all hands on deck. That is enough.

Am I suggesting that we are ever and always at sea, never to shelter in a safe harbor? No. Sometimes we have to immediately point our boats in the direction of a safe harbor—especially when we have been battered and bruised. "There's no need to be a hero," as my mami used to say. We enter a safe harbor when we need to rest. We stay awhile. It is not God's will that we burn out. Jesus took time to rest—even in boats! Christians especially need to learn how to be still and know that God is God. Sabbath. Go to lonely places and pray, like Jesus did. Otherwise, we will burn out, making ourselves and everyone around us miserable. We need not give in to those who guilt us or cajole us into leaving safe havens before we are ready. The problem comes when we try to stay in a safe harbor when it is time to depart. It's when we pull a Jonah and flee to Tarshish, refusing to go to Nineveh (Jonah 1:1-3). If you recall, I was once asking the Lord to let me be in a safe harbor for a long time, to speak to the storms that came my way so that the winds and the waves in my life would calm down and I could remain for a long time. And he gently reminded me that staying in the harbor isn't what boats are for.

It is hard to see in storms. Sometimes it's downright impossible. So we hold on for dear life to Jesus in us.

It is important to note this concerning our life: Seldom, if ever, will we know anything until we take the next step. After praying about the next thing for us and seeking guidance, we need to know that insight or enlightenment about a situation comes *after* we take the next step, not *before*. It makes sense, doesn't it? We can think about Jesus all the time, knowing what the Bible and church teach about him, but until we trust him, nothing will change. When it comes to discernment, we can contemplate it all we want and have heightened awareness about what we must do, but we will not truly know deep down in our soul, and nothing will change, until we take concrete steps. *Do. Know (deep down). Become.*

LED THROUGH OUR END

We shall not cease from exploration
And the end of all our exploring
Will be to arrive where we started
And know the place for the first time.

T. S. ELIOT

WHEN WE LIVE OUT OF OUR JOYS AND LOVES, it is incumbent on us that we do whatever we can to make the same thing possible for everyone.

Is all this "God's will" talk just for the middle- and upper-class people of the world who have the means to obey? I don't think so. Jesus himself was poor—so poor after starting ministry that he said he had "no place to lay his head" (Matthew 8:20). Many of the saints we know of had very little.

Impossibilities

Maybe we believe what God is calling us to do is nearly impossible. Perhaps we are impoverished, without the means to do what we believe he wants us to do. We have no time. We work hard all day just to survive and are barely doing it.

Knowing and following God's will is not just for the well-off of the world. The same truths apply to the rural village person living up high in the Andes or Himalayan mountains. To folks in the poorest parts of Appalachia. To the lower castes in the slums of India. To my South African friends, who are still suffering the effects of apartheid, having to drink polluted water from upstream, where chemicals, animal feces, and urine carry diseases to them because of the corrupt system that strips them of their land and resources while they work as almost enslaved.

Wherever we are on the earth, God is near; he is with us and in us, guiding us. Growing up poor in the US, I knew that God was near and I could follow his will for me. But the poverty here is wealth compared to that in other parts of the world. I do not have the answer to the problem of evil. No one does. But I do believe that God does not kick us when we are down—"a bruised reed he will not break" (Isaiah 42:3). In the Kingdom, many of the first will be last, and many of the last will be first (Matthew 19:30).

Economic constraints and limitations are one kind of impossibility. Another kind of impossibility is in our imaginations. For example, we have been outright told or led to believe that we can never do this or that because we are of a certain race or gender. There are corrupt social and political forces acting on us all, and those forces are found in, and tragically often perpetuated by, the church. And one lamentable result of this cultural captivity is people who simply can't imagine—due to their identity and social and political location—that a certain way of life or path in the world is available to them or even *meant* for them. We're left to wonder just how many lives throughout history and around the world have been shipwrecked because of this— far too many people who have been severely discouraged or prohibited from pursuing God's call on their lives due to the suffocating prejudicial environments in which they've lived.

One specific example is women in certain Christian circles who have been told that to be a good and faithful Christian woman, one has only a limited range of options: be a wife, mother, Sunday school teacher, and/or missionary. They are not to work outside the home, they've been told, because that is not fulfilling God's will for them as a woman.

We have no idea how God can pull off what we believe he is calling us to do. What happens when our backs are up against the wall? What happens when we feel trapped? Maybe we panicked and made bad decisions and now feel like we cannot get out of them. Like that ship has sailed. We might not be able to do what we want to do, like marry that person we initially dismissed. Now we realize our error, but they are married to someone else.

God will never turn his back on us. And so we pray. And then we trust and wait. There's no way around it. Meanwhile, we prepare to act the moment the way opens. We do our part and wait for God to do his part. I have seen God do more than I could ever ask for or imagine (Ephesians 3:20) too many times—but never on my timetable. May we surround ourselves with people who will pray and help us believe, and may we ask God to help our unbelief (Mark 9:23-25).

There's no need to wait to make good decisions. We do not have to pray about whether we should seek help for alcoholism, stop mistreating people, or get out of a toxic situation. We are always to choose life, that which is life-giving in Christ, whatever is true and good and beautiful, and never that which is death-dealing or evil (Philippians 4:8). That is God's will. Sometimes we wrongfully delay by saying we will pray about something when really fear or habit is what is keeping us from doing what we need to do, from sailing in the direction of God's will.

What are we to say about people whose lives are hell on earth? When raising challenges to certain dominant views of meaning in life, my husband poses this question to his students: "What about people who were trafficked on slave ships and who experienced the catastrophic abuse and oppression of the Middle Passage? Should they have been told to pursue their passions, to find fulfillment, to live out of their loves and joys, their identities?" How can people embrace who they are when they literally cannot *be* who they are—when they have little to no agency, little to no freedom to *be*, to *go*, to *do*, and to *be with*? How does all this work out for those who are bought, sold, used, and abused as property? For those children who are trafficked and exploited? For those who have been brutalized and maimed by war and violence?

Through no fault of their own, they are not situated well

to listen to their lives or to pay attention. Are their lives meaningless? Absolutely not. They are caught in the wickedness and injustice of the world—in the theft, murder, and destruction unleashed by the devil and his demons and perpetuated by us, often in perverse pursuit of power and profit.

What is God thinking? I do not have all the answers. But I do know that God is for them. And I know this: A lot of their suffering is on us. On us! This is where we return to Saint Antony's word: "From the neighbour comes life and death."[1] We cannot in good conscience call ourselves Christians and not lay our lives down for the flourishing of others. That is an essential, nonnegotiable part of our journey.

Go This Way

We cooperate with God, freely surrendering to the direction of the Spirit—or not. God will not force us to do his will. Love is not coercive and controlling. But God promises this to each of us as we walk in him, listen to him, and love him: "Whether you turn to the right or to the left, your ears will hear a voice behind you, saying, 'This is the way; walk in it'" (Isaiah 30:21).

Going out to sea is a metaphor for embracing God's will for our lives. We pay close attention, discovering instructions for navigation, the weather, and our destination so that God's will may be done on earth as it is in heaven.

If we believe, as Dallas Willard said, that the Kingdom of God is the safest place to be, then we can go out to sea in peace and with expectation. We can go out to sea to live and serve as Jesus rests and relaxes in our lives, in our boats. Hopefully he will be able to get comfortable.

Mami died sometime between 2:30 and 4:00 a.m. on Sunday, June 27, 2021. I had left her at midnight so I could spend the night at my brother Marco's house. I'd stayed in the room with her for days on end but then had started staying with Marco and Shelly when Kenny and Chelsea had arrived with their family from Georgia. The house was crowded. Before I left, I kissed her and repeatedly said, "You are the love of my life." Kenny, Chelsea, and my sister, Michelle, were all sleeping in the room with her.

That night, it was Chelsea who happened to wake up and check to make sure Mami was comfortable. She noticed that Mami's chest was no longer rising and falling. She was gone. The call I dreaded and knew was coming came. Chelsea called us a little after 4:00 a.m., and we arrived not too long after.

When we arrived, Mami was still warm. And when we all looked at her, we gazed at her in amazement. She was looking up to the heavens with a little smile. Until then, she had been in incredible pain, and the pain had been written all over her face (although throughout the sickness she remained ever sweet and kind). Here we were in the wee hours of a Sunday morning, and we saw peace, an everything-is-right-with-the-world look. Mami's journey among us in our waters was over. The angels had come and borne her up to heaven, her destination. We could see it on her face.

I came close to death once. It was when I was delivering

We can go out to sea to live and serve as Jesus rests and relaxes in our lives, in our boats. Hopefully he will be able to get comfortable.

our youngest daughter, Isabella. Midway through the delivery, the doctors discovered an issue with my blood platelets—they weren't clotting the way they should. That meant that I could hemorrhage. Bleed out during delivery. I knew something was wrong when the SWAT team came into my room and I saw a look of great concern on Shawn's face. By "SWAT team," I mean a team of about twenty nurses and doctors who crowded into the otherwise good-sized delivery room.

I asked my doctor, "Can't I have any medication to help with my labor pains?" "No," he said. "It could paralyze you." "Well, then, am I to have a C-section?" "That's too dangerous." "What if I bleed out in my natural delivery?" "We'll give you a blood transfusion," he said. It turns out that no matter what it was dangerous.

The medical SWAT team was there to administer medicine and care because of the real possibility that I could lose too much blood. I could not stop the process. Isabella had to come out naturally. Then the seriousness of the situation hit me. There was a real possibility I could die in childbirth. I now knew why I was seeing concern on the faces around me.

But on the heels of that realization, I had perfect peace. The peace that is beyond understanding fell on me. Internally I said to the Lord, *You have never failed me once. And I know you won't fail me now. Yea, though I walk through the valley of the shadow of death, your rod and staff shall comfort me. I know you will take care of me.* And then I prayed, *Lord, if I don't make it, please let Isabella live. Please take care of Shawn and the girls. That's all.* Indeed, peace blanketed my soul. It was not a peace that I had to conjure up. It was otherworldly, heavenly. I knew God was with me even if I were to pass from life here, through the curtain of death, and into the rest of my life—eternal life.

One day, we will make our last voyage here. And God will be with us. He will send his angels to bear us up and show us the way. I believe that beyond a shadow of a doubt. We bear Jesus in our boats, and he bears our boats into paradise with him. We will be at peace. On that final day and moment of our voyage, he will utter to us, "Today you will be with me in paradise" (Luke 23:43).

Acknowledgments

Mami died at the height of the COVID-19 pandemic, so I did not have much of the physical presence or the hugs from local friends and church family I normally would have had. That was hard. In fact, some did not even know that Mami had died until much later because personal announcements were no longer made on Sunday mornings to our church family for privacy reasons, given that anyone could be watching online. It was part of the physical detachment we all experienced because of the global pandemic.

However, I did have much love sent from afar. Facebook messages, email messages. Many friends, even social-media friends I have never met in person, sent us meals and cards and gas money while we were taking care of Mami in hospice. That all meant the world to me and my family. So thank you to all of you who cared for us from near and far during a raging pandemic—many of you are readers turned friends! My siblings and I truly could not have physically loved Mami well until the end of her life here on earth without your comfort and material help. You are my friends and family scattered to the four winds and are precious to me.

The deepest of gratitude goes to Shawn, who parented mostly alone for eight months while I was in school and drove back and forth across state lines to care for Mami in a rotation with my siblings—Marco, Michelle, and Kenny—and my sisters-in-law— Shelly and Chelsea. Shawn has always gone above and beyond; he is quintessentially Christian, the best father a person could be to our three daughters, and the best husband I could ask for. I adore him. Iliana, Valentina, and Isabella—thank you for understanding that I was taking care of Abuelita while in my PhD program. That year was extremely hard, and I was gone a lot. I adore you and love you.

Dad, Marco, Kenny, Michelle, Shelly, and Chelsea: I thank God repeatedly for you. I thank God that we get to have the close, wonderful family we have here on earth and, I trust, in heaven with Mami. I get to be with you in all dimensions! With Shawn, you have always been my biggest fans, and I hope you know I am yours. We have known loving family in this world despite difficulty. What a gift. I cry while thanking God for his goodness in giving you all to me. We were in our own little world for almost a year caring for Mami, and I will never forget it. And Mami, I love you more than you'll ever know.

Thank you, Grandma Trudy, for loving us in so many ways, and for loving us and the girls concretely. Your love for us is a treasure, and we all love you.

To Nanny and Carl, our friends/family—we love you deeply and rejoice in your love for us and the girls. You are the best!

As always, thank you to our pastors: Russ, Joanie, and now Barry. Your love and influence bears great fruit. You don't even know. Thank you to our church family at Maumee United Methodist. We will miss you.

I also want to give special thanks to our friends David and Rachel Barkholz, who are hilarious and fun and were often chauffeurs to our youngest two while I wrote this book and was in school and traveling. When Shawn could not be in two places at once, you generously and kindly picked up the slack. The world and our family are better because of you.

Thank you to my peers in my PhD cohort and my professors in the American Culture Studies program at Bowling Green State University for your kindness and love and support. What a terrific program full of gracious and brilliant people! I have learned a lot from you.

God's grace has found me in that I get to have the job of my dreams: professor of spiritual formation at Northeastern Seminary on the campus of Roberts Wesleyan University. All my coworkers are amazing. What an honor.

And to you, readers: I would not be here without you. I would love to hear what you think about the things in these pages.

Finally, I am grateful to NavPress and the friends at Tyndale for bringing this project together. Many thanks to David Zimmerman for taking a risk on me! And deepest thanks to my editor, Deborah Gonzalez, for her enthusiasm and support for this book. My thanks also go to copy editor Elizabeth Schroll for her keen eye and quick wit in catching my writing missteps. This book is better because of her! And to my agent, Christopher Ferebee—you are amazing at what you do!

About the Author

Marlena Graves is the assistant professor of spiritual formation at Northeastern Seminary on the campus of Roberts Wesleyan University. She has written five books and a significant number of articles that can be found in a variety of venues. She has been interviewed by such outlets as Reuters, *The New Yorker*, and RELEVANT. She is a regular guest on podcasts and often speaks to students, congregations, organizations, and retreat groups about life in God. She adores her husband, Shawn, a philosophy professor, and their three daughters. She likes anything to do with Puerto Rico, laughing, dancing, going to monasteries, and being out in nature. She and her family live in the Rochester, New York, area.

Notes

CHAPTER 1 | JOURNEY WITH JESUS INTO UNCHARTED WATERS
1. William Ernest Henley, "Invictus," Poetry Foundation, accessed September 9, 2022, https://www.poetryfoundation.org/poems/51642/invictus.

CHAPTER 2 | LED BY LOVE OF GOD AND NEIGHBOR
1. The Flamingos, "I Only Have Eyes for You," *Flamingos Serenade* © 1959 End Records. This song was written in 1934 (music by Harry Warren, lyrics by Al Dubin) but became more well known when the Flamingos popularized it in 1959.
2. Dorothy Day, *The Long Loneliness: The Autobiography of Dorothy Day* (New York: HarperCollins, 1997), 107.
3. "The great thing, if one can, is to stop regarding all the unpleasant things as interruptions of one's 'own,' or 'real' life. The truth is of course that what one calls the interruptions are precisely one's real life—the life God is sending one day by day: what one calls one's 'real life' is a phantom of one's own imagination. This at least is what I see at moments of insight: but it's hard to remember it all the time." Walter Hooper, ed., *They Stand Together: The Letters of C. S. Lewis to Arthur Greeves, 1914–1963* (London: Collins, 1979), 499.
4. Ewelina U. Ochab, "Remembering the 21 Coptic Orthodox Christians Murdered by Daesh," *Forbes*, February 14, 2019, https://www.forbes.com/sites/ewelinaochab/2019/02/14/remembering-the-21-coptic-orthodox-christians-murdered-by-daesh/?sh=3211f3ef4dcf.
5. "We can do no great things—only small things with great love." *Love, a Fruit Always in Season: Daily Meditations from the Words of Mother Teresa of Calcutta*, ed. Dorothy S. Hunt (San Francisco: Ignatius Press, 1989), 121.
6. John Cougar, "Jack and Diane," *American Fool* © 1982 Riva Records.

7. Nicole Frehsee, "'We Can't Have All Our Artists Die': How the Music Industry Is Fighting the Mental-Health Crisis," *Rolling Stone*, January 21, 2020, https://www.rollingstone.com/music/music-features/we-cant-have-all-our-artists-die-how-the-music-industry-is-fighting-the-mental-health-crisis-939171.

8. As quoted in Samuel Rubenson, *The Letters of St. Antony: Monasticism and the Making of a Saint* (Minneapolis: Fortress, 1995), 222.

9. As quoted in Rubenson, *Letters of St. Antony*, 155.

CHAPTER 3 | LED BY OUR LOVES AND JOYS

1. Irenaeus, *A Treatise against the Heresies*, Book IV.

2. Julian of Norwich, *Revelations of Divine Love*, trans. Barry Windeatt (New York: Oxford University Press, 2015), 74.

3. Parker J. Palmer, *Let Your Life Speak: Listening for the Voice of Vocation* (San Francisco: Jossey-Bass, 2000), 97.

CHAPTER 4 | LED BY OUR PLACE

1. C. S. Lewis, *The Magician's Nephew*, The Chronicles of Narnia (New York: HarperTrophy, 1994), 148.

2. Rowan Williams, *Where God Happens: Discovering Christ in One Another* (Boston: New Seed Books, 2005), 24.

3. Gregory Boyle, *Tattoos on the Heart: The Power of Boundless Compassion* (New York: Free Press, 2010), 133.

4. Boyle, *Tattoos*, 136–37.

5. Boyle, *Tattoos*, 139.

6. "Sometimes you want to go where everybody knows your name / And they're always glad you came." Gary Portnoy and Judy Hart Angelo, "Theme from *Cheers* (Where Everybody Knows Your Name)" / "Jenny" (single) © 1983 Earthtone.

7. Marlena Graves, *The Way Up Is Down: Becoming Yourself by Forgetting Yourself* (Downers Grove, IL: IVP, 2020).

CHAPTER 5 | LED BY DISCERNMENT

1. See, for example, https://www.mic.com/articles/87851/11-popular-songs-the-cia-used-to-torture-prisoners-in-the-war-on-terror.

2. See, for example, https://www.vox.com/2018/4/18/17168504/restaurants-noise-levels-loud-decibels.

3. Knvul Sheikh, "Noise Pollution Isn't Just Annoying—It's Bad for Your Health," BrainFacts.org, June 27, 2018, https://www.brainfacts.org/thinking

-sensing-and-behaving/diet-and-lifestyle/2018/noise-pollution-isnt-just
-annoying-its-bad-for-your-health-062718.

4. Francis Scott Key, "The Star-Spangled Banner," 1814. Public domain.

5. Brad Pitt as Tyler Durden, *Fight Club* (Los Angeles: Twentieth Century Fox, 1999).

6. Parker J. Palmer, *Let Your Life Speak: Listening for the Voice of Vocation* (San Francisco: Jossey-Bass, 2000), 38.

7. Palmer, *Let Your Life Speak*, 38.

8. Palmer, *Let Your Life Speak*, 38.

9. Palmer, *Let Your Life Speak*, 39.

10. Richard Sherman and Robert B. Sherman, "A Spoonful of Sugar." First performed by Julie Andrews in the movie musical *Mary Poppins* (Burbank, CA: Walt Disney, 1964).

CHAPTER 6 | LED THROUGH OUR END

1. See chapter 2, note 9.

Read as a group!

A digital leader's guide with discussion
questions is available here.